IT'S NEVER TOO LATE FOR GOD TO MOVE

Dr. Lillie P. Gray

authorHOUSE®

AuthorHouse™
1663 Liberty Drive
Bloomington, IN 47403
www.authorhouse.com
Phone: 1-800-839-8640

First published by AuthorHouse 9/1/2011

ISBN: 978-1-4567-2094-0 (sc)
ISBN: 978-1-4567-2093-3 (e)

Contents

ACKNOWLEDGEMENT

My gratitude to all who has helped me in this book. Thank you Missionary Joyce Hubbard for your enthusiasm, encouragement, wisdom and for believing in my messages and methods.

Thank you Evangelist Sandra Porter who became a pillar in the completion of what God has given me through the years, "A Word for the Lord".

To write the anointed words that God has given me to help others, it has been a joy in hearing and heeding to the voice of God. I give God all the Glory, Honor and Praise for being the vessel that he used for such time as this.

Thanks to Mr. Harold Nichols for all the graphics and time spent in helping me designed my book cover and pictures.

Habakkuk 2:1,2 says, I will stand upon my watch, and set me upon the tower, and will watch to see what he will say unto me, and what I shall answer when I am reproved. And the Lord answered me, and said, Write the vision, and make it plain upon tables, that he may run that readeth it.

There are many tools others may use in the message written. Be Encourage through these messages for God. *PRAISE GOD*

Ephesians 5:20 Giving thanks always for all things unto God ad the Father in the name of our Lord Jesus Christ.

PRAYERS

I will bless the Lord at all times: his praises shall continually be in my mouth. (Ps. 34:1)

O magnify the Lord with me and let us exalt his name together. (Ps. 34:3)

O taste and see that the Lord is good, blessed is the man that trusteth in him. (Ps. 34:8)

For the Lord loved judgment, and forsaketh not his saints, they are preserved for ever: but the seed of the wicked shall be cut off. (Ps. 37:28)

Moreover whom he did predestinate, them he also called: and whom he called, them he also justified: and whom he justified, them he also glorified. (Romans 8:30)

The Lord has always answered my prayers and given me direction for my life. He dwells in me and I know his voice. Even through difficult times, he has shown me the way and I can see the results. The Lord will word your mouth and the Holy Spirit will confirm it all you have to do is stand on his word and let him speak through you. "For I the Lord thy God will hold thy right hand, saying unto thee, fear not; I will help thee." (Isa. 41:13)

In Closing, thank you father that I can be absolutely sure you will never leave me or forsake me because I am in Christ Jesus.

TO
The memory of my brother
Bishop W. L. Porter

He was a great asset to my accomplishment in my success of my life.
A man of faith to follow.

June 18, 1924 - April 11, 2009

My brother was a great asset to many accomplishments and the
success of my life. He was a role model, my pastor, an adviser for me
and my family, a caretaker in my younger years, and a friend. He
developed many significant programs that are still being utilized
today in the National Church of God in Christ. He started the
first housing department for delegates' from all over the world and
organized the first transportation department. His accomplishments
included, Superintendent of National Properties; Tennessee Central
Ecclesiastical Jurisdictional Bishop and elected General Board
Member. With the help of God, he was a great achiever.

YOU MEANT SO MUCH TO ME

SOME
PEOPLE ARE
ALWAYS
CLOSE IN HEART

So often things get in the way
Of all we really want to say
To those whose thoughtful ways
We treasure so….

We're grateful for the times they've cared
The comfort and advice they've shared
Yet, sometimes find it hard
To let them know…

But they will always be a part
Of all we hold so close in heart,
For they mean more
Than words could ever show.

You always find a way
To help me out, to give and share,
You always find the time
To talk awhile, to just be there,
And though I may not always
Find the words to show I care,
I hope, within your heart,
You'll always know.

Bishop Porter

DAVID PORTER

SONGWRITER/PRODUCER
DAVID PORTER ENTERPRISES, INC.

FROM MY BROTHER:

*L*illie Pearl Porter is first my blood sister. Many people know her as Dr. Lillie P. Gray, but to me she is my sister, who I love very much. This lady who is so widely respected, she is first a caring mother, grandmother, aunt, cousin and sister, that is highly looked up to in her family. She has a long history of being a giver in the Porter family. The early years of my life I can remember her as the role model for the success that all of us aspired to attain. She was never selfish in giving the full family the tools to feel that we were a part of even her early success. She was the motivation to the other brothers and sisters, that we to could have a better life by working hard and staying focused with set goals.

Now, years later, as I look at her many accomplishments in her role as a Minister, Educator, Entrepreneur, Servant and her shining examples of how it can be done. I can't help but be extremely proud and happy for her. I smile when I think back to the 1970's when I produced a song idea that my sister came up with call, "Love Tempo" and it was placed on wax for release and she became a signed BMI songwriter. *So now you see, she even got on to my turf.*

Dr. Lillie P. Gray has two brother who were Bishops of the cloth, a brother who is a hall of fame songwriter and producer, other brothers and sisters who have all made great strides, who would to the last say, "you are to us a SUPERSTAR and we love you so and are tremendously proud of your many, many accomplishments."

I'm proud to say, you are our sister, We LOVE you now and forever.

David Porter, Stax Records, *songwriter/producer*

MOTHER'S LOVE

How sweet a Mother's Love
How gentle her ways
How tender her smiles
And arms that embrace our days.

How sweet a Mother's Love
That carries us through
Many trials and tribulations
And always say " I Love You"

How sweet a Mother's Love
That reaches out for us
And reminds us of
The love that comes from Thee

How sweet a Mother's Love
That nurtures us night and day
Never yielding, never fading
Never, never going away

We will always praise the Lord
With Prayer and Faith
You taught us all that
With caring love and embrace.

We serve and On-time God

Thank you, MOM

Your daughter,
Jackie

DEDICATION

For a grandmother who blessed my life in so many ways.
Thanks you for your "Guidance", for encouraging me
to know my own worth. To have enough faith in
my self to leave no room for self doubt.

"Wisdom" for teaching me how to think for my self
and make decisions on what is right, rather
than what is easy in "Grace".

For showing me how to be humble and recognize that
although I am somebody it's not always about me.

"Dignity"
For creating in me a strong foundation so
I can understand where I come from and to
be confident in where I am going.
And most of all Thank you for your heart.
For being like a mother to me so that I have
always known what it feels like
to be accepted, valued, and completely loved.

With all my heart I love you, Grandmother.

Love Markey (Keddie) Granberry

FOREWORD

"IT'S NEVER TO LATE FOR GOD TO MOVE"

*I*s a word from the lord, many inspired messages that was written through the inspiration of the leading of the Lord. Based on the Bible and clear and persuasive statements of Christian positions.

Each volume is personalize by its author. The author will show the vitality of Christian doctrines and their meaning for everyday life.

Strong and fresh illustrations will hold the interest of the reader.

Some are the personal faith of the author.

"Whom he did predestinate then he also called and whom he called then he also justified: and who he justified then he also glorified." Romans 8:30

THROUGH TOUGH TIMES
GOD DIRECTED MY LIFE
FROM THE GHETTO

was born in Memphis, Tennessee. We lived in rented housing surrounded by low esteem. My mother had a child every two years. I was the fourth child; there were three other brothers before me. At the age of eight I became a surrogate parent and didn't know the role as they arrived I became a helper for my mother to care for them. Washing, cleaning and household chores my experience was out of content for a child. My father worked for IC Railroad as a switchman engine. I had to do adult chores as well as a child I was placed in an adult position. Times were not good, there was very little money to care for the family, but I had a good father, he did the best he could for us. His sisters would help to support us with clothing. I recall one aunt worked for a wealthy family that had twins and they donated their good clothing to us.

My father carried me to church I remember when I received salvation at age eleven years old. I always loved church and school. I remember when I was about eight years old; it was on a Sunday very cold and ice was on the ground the streets was slick and I wanted to attend Sunday school, my mother was reluctant about me falling. I convinced her I would be alright, I didn't have any galosh for my shoes to protect my feet. Therefore, she cut a cloth sack and tied it on my feet and I went to church. I can say at a young age God was preparing me for my destiny. We lived in a small house with plumbing outside the home and when it rained we had our own swimming pool. Cole manufacturing was at the back of the house and there was a fence, we would climb under it and get wood out so we would have wood for heat. I recall a man who worked there name Mr. Richard. For lunch, his wife prepared sauer kraut and hotdogs for him every day, but he would give it to us.

We were a close knit family. We were taught to love one another and always pray that God would provide for us. I was the oldest girl of twelve siblings. I help nuture the younger children therefore I grew up at an early age. I was a helper for my mother who was having babies and needed assistance. As the years went by my father became ill and Dr. A. T. Martin was treating him for indigestion They called the railroad doctor from Chicago and he came to see him and was sent to Collins Chapel Hospital. He died within a week. I recall that I always had a mind for business. When I became old enough I went to an attorney because he was given the wrong diagnosis for his illness. I had a case but it was over the statute of limitation. Times became where as my mother told me at age sixteen she could no longer afford to send me to school. I always love getting an education. A young man asked me to marry me and would see that I received my education. They talked me into the ideal of marrying I was not aware of anything expected from a wife. I was not educated in that area of life. So I did marry and completed my high school education on time with my class. My brother went with me to get married. To me it was a joke with no experience. Heb. 12:2

REFLECTIONS OF MY LIFE

I was working in a toy factory running a machine making bow and arrows. One day the Lord spoke to me and said this is not where you belong. I immediately stopped and went to speak with the supervisor and told him I wanted to go back to school he encouraged me to pursue my goal. In fact, he offered to assist with my education. I started at Rust College in Holly Spring, Mississippi and two of my closes friends attend school with me. I was a role model for two other ladies who also worked in the factory with me. They went back to school and they became educators. You never know who is watching you.

Attending college increase my ability to learn and desire more knowledge. I was able to change careers. I worked one year for the Board of Education in the Memphis Recreation Department as a clerk typist. Later, I applied for a clerk typist position at Atlanta Life Insurance company and I worked there for eight years. One day LT. General George W. Lee, who was one of the presidents of Atlanta Life Insurance Company, called me into his office and politely asked me to have a seat. He stated, "I have been observing your work ethics, a woman of your caliber will always be successful." Those words have been a motivating force in my life to let nothing hinder my thought process of what I can achieve in life. When he spoke to me that morning his words germinate inside of me to act on what he said.

Once again, another great man saw potential in me.

I remember when my third child Belinda finished high school, she stated to me, " I am not going to attend college after graduating from high school this year." I said to her, "Oh! You are not?" I took all her information and identification and enrolled her into Memphis State University to start her freshmen year. Upon returning home, I told her that" she was a student at Memphis State University." she was amazed at my action. She soon became excited about the idea of attending college and she began to prepare herself to achieve her goals. Belinda and I were Sociology majors under the guidance of Dr. Andy Fox. She attended day classes and in the same year, I attended night classes and had the same instructor. Due to the lack of time span and years lost in my childhood getting an education was important and is the foundation for growth. Being a divorced woman with three children I was determined that my children would have an opportunity to get an education with my support.

IT'S NEVER TOO LATE

It's never too late
It's mind over matter.
Who are you going to let win

And does it matter?
Press forward to a higher calling-
Because it does matter to reach
our heights in life.

We know that what we do does matter-
To seek better things for your good.
It's never too late and it does matter.

Lillie P. Gray

MY DESTINY

God had my destiny in his hands, there were times my brothers and sisters didn't understand me but I knew God had a calling on my life to be used of him.

Jesus bore our sins that we might be saved. There is a price you have to pay and you will be misunderstood when God choose you.

"A word from God" beginning 1974. I would let my brother Bishop Claude Porter, P.H.D., who is the pastor of Proviso Baptist Church and Proviso Leyden Council a community action program in Maywood, IL. preach my sermons for ten years before I accepted my calling from the Lord.

I attended Mason Bible College in 1984 and was licensed by the Church Of God In Christ (C.O.G.I.C.) as an Evangelist Missionary. I worked beside my brother Bishop W. L. Porter, Prelate of Central Tennessee C.O.G.I.C. as the Assistant Director of the National Housing Department for C.O.G.I.C., placing delegates in hotels across the city and everywhere we could find accommodations in Arkansas, Mississippi, and Tennessee. Also, I worked with the late Bishop German Ross in the Registration Department, Bishop J. O. Paterson Sr. during the Holy Ghost Conference for the National Church.

After resigning from the National Housing Department in 1997, I went back to school. I completed my Masters Degree in Theology. On May 18, 2002 I received my Doctorate Degree in Religious Philosophy in Christian Counseling and was ordained as an Evangelist by the Jacksonville Theological Seminary.

The year I attended Jacksonville Seminary, Belinda attended school with me and she received her BS Degree and was licensed as a Minister.

God did just what he planned for my life in the ministry. I am yet seeking to be used of God where ever he leads me. I made a covenant with God, who leads me into all truth. Lord God, I pray that you may count me worthy of your calling and that by power you may fulfill every good purpose of mine and every act by my faith.

Father God, like Timothy's grandmother Lois, and his mother Eunice, help me to pass down a heritage of faith. Lord God, you have chosen these who are poor in the eyes of the world to be rich in faith and to inherit the kingdom you promised those who love you (II Thess. 1:-5). I just want to say "yes to God" (James 2:5).

MY PERSONAL TESTIMONY

God will keep his promise if you keep his commandments. We are a chosen generation in the royal priesthood of God. Our destiny is in God's hands. He has full control of our lives.

I received salvation at a very early age. I became totally committed to God in 1974 when I realized he had a calling on my life. I didn't fully accept the task until 1984. I received the Baptism of the Holy Ghost, which was the keeping power for me. I would write sermons and my brother, who also pastored a church in Maywood, Illinois preached them. I wrote a sermon, "Train Ride To Glory" and was edified with the Holy Ghost with the anointing and speaking of tongues as he gave me utterance. This happened when my family and I visited my brother's church. We were there for a family reunion.

We are the body of Christ. We must abide in his word and do the perfect will of the Father, which is in heaven. I chose to live for God and follow his direction. God gave me a special anointing of 'laying on hands' on the sick and pray for many.

One experience I had was with a young man. He had been shot in the stomach and was expected to die. I called my daughter and she stated that he would not make it through the night. I told them to inform his mother that I would be there to pray for him. I arrived at the hospital and went to the trauma unit. He was awake so I told him even though he couldn't speak, he could use his mind to ask God for mercy and deliverance out of his situation.

I told him to bat his eyes if he understood what I was saying and he did. I prayed for him asked the Lord to heal him and give him another chance. The anointing came as I touched him, I asked God to let us see a miracle by morning. The life support machine was on him with tubes hanging from every side of him. They had not sewn up the gunshot wound in his stomach. As I prayed, I turned and grabbed the nurse's hand and told her that the Lord was going to use her for a point of contact and prayed with her and told her to expect a miracle by morning. I told him to continue to use his mind to pray. Remember they had left him there to die. But God said no.

I received a call at 6 a.m. from the nurse at the hospital saying, "We received our miracle." He was disconnected from all life support and tubes and sitting up on the side of the bed. That's how God works. He can turn it around. When man gives in he takes over, if it is his will.

I told Keith, the next day, that God had given him another chance but he wants something in return. That was his life. He would be a vessel he could use to witness that God had saved his life. I told him, if he didn't obey and follow the principle of God, he would not last. Only what you do for Christ will last. He was released from the hospital completely healed.

"God is the one that healeth thee. I partition thy throne of grace to receive the healing through me as standing in the gap".

In another instance, I was called by one of my daughters saying they had flown one of her co-worker into Memphis because had a stroke and asked me to go to the hospital and pray for her. I didn't know her but God did. I went to Methodist Central Hospital Intensive Care Unit on the second floor and asked the nurse to show me the young lady that was flown in from Alabama. I was given directions to where she was. I found her unconscious with a fan on her to help cool her body temperature. She was on life support and had tubes everywhere. I told the Lord that I was standing in the gap to be used by him. He knew all about her and he could turn it around. I prayed and the anointing came and I knew God heard my prayer. I left the hospital and called my daughter and informed her that I had prayed for her friend and she was in the Lord's hand to be delivered.

Two weeks later, I received a call from my daughter telling me her friend was out of intensive care, talking and had all of her faculties. I asked my daughter to take me to visit her. We went to the hospital to see her and she was amazed at who I was. I explained to her that I was the guardian angel that God sent to pray for her. She was very receptive and thankful. She fully recovered after being released from the hospital.

I was a guardian angel for my sister-in-law. The feeling came upon me that something was wrong with my sister-in-law. I informed the person in my office that I had to leave. I drove to her home and found her car in the driveway. She was an educator with the city school system in a top management position. But she had a drinking problem. She would buy liquor by the case. There was no activity around the house. I rang the doorbell and no one answered. I went to the back door and knocked, no answer. I decided to go to her bedroom window and call her name. I could hear her trying to answer me with a very faint voice and I knew she was in trouble. Immediately, I went to a neighbor and told her my findings and placed a call to 911. The firemen came within minutes. They wanted to break down her door, but I asked them to use the back window and removed the bars from the den window for the small fireman to enter.

We found her in the bedroom on the floor between the bed and the nightstand. She was lying in her own urine and feces. She didn't understand anything. They rushed her to the hospital and placed her in intensive care for thirty days before she could be moved to a regular room in the hospital. God had intervened and placed me there for this crisis to save her life. She didn't understand why she was there and how she got there. "How did you know?" she asked. I told her, "The Lord sent me. I followed his Spirit and promised him I would go wherever he sends me." I told her I was her guardian angel.

God uses ordinary people to heed his call and his purpose.

'In all thy ways acknowledge him and he shall direct thy paths (Proverbs 3:6)."

My brother became very ill and was placed in the hospital for two and a half weeks before they told us that he was not going to recover. We were called to hospital at 4 a.m. one morning because all his vital signs were leaving. My daughter and I began to pray and rebuke death. The Lord heard us and my brother came out of that crisis and was able to talk with us. The next two weeks he was sent home to die; he had made his peace with God. I led him in prayer daily. During his transition, I was holding his hands and he was holding on to me. He knew he was dying but stayed in good spirit. As he was crossing over he told me he smelled flowers. I asked, "What kind?" And he said, "Yellow roses." I asked him did he see a bed of them? He said, "Yes." I told him to tell the Lord thanks because the Lord is a sweet smelling Savior and squeeze my hand. He did very quickly and he was gone. That was a great feeling to know that God made his presence known. I know that God had received his spirit and I am grateful he gave me that experience. My daughter and nephew were standing outside of the house and they witnessed the light coming down from the sky to the house to receive my brother's spirit. Praise God!

We are the body of Christ. We must abide in his word and do his will. The will of God, His perfect will. Not of ourselves, but only his Holy Spirit which guides us in the direction of holiness. God knows our every thought before we speak.

Therefore we must be careful in our subconscious to keep a clean spirit and stay prayerful at all times.

When we read his word, that's when he's watering our soul to keep in divine will. By living by his word. He will give us everlasting life. "Thy word have I hid in my mine heart, that I might not sin against thee (Psalm 119:11). " We are the sheep of his pasture and he is our shepherd.

Another Victorious Testimony

Angelia Porter, my sister-in-law, was very ill in Methodist Hospital in 2003. She had a heart attack, was diagnosed with a congestive heart failure and was in a coma. I laid hands on her and begin to pray for a miracle and the Lord heard my prayer. She began to make a noise as if she was clearing her throat. She came out of the coma and after several days, she was sent home. God showed himself with her life, giving her another chance.

Praise God!

Hallelujah!

Praise God!

A Word From The Lord

He awoke me one morning at 3 a.m. and told me that he had called me, not man, into the ministry. He shall work many miracles in my life. I will know much jealousy around me, but don't worry. He will raise me above my adversaries. He will place a hedge around me for a safety net. I shall witness to many about his goodness in my life. "Ye shall be blessed and your seeds seed shall be blessed. Ye shall be blessed in your going and your coming," saith the Lord.

Being confident of this very thing, that he which hath begun a good work in you will perform it until the day of Jesus Christ" (Philippians 1:6).

"JUST SAY YES"

Yes I am Somebody
Yes I will refuse drugs
Yes I will tell the truth
Yes I will Survive
Yes I do have a chance
Yes because as of today
I will make a Stand.

When you get to heaven, be sure
To bring your MasterCard
Because GOD don't take the
Devil's Express.

"At the Break of Dawn"

At the break of dawn a new day has begun.
At the break of dawn the stars cease to shine.

At the break of dawn a babe is born, and new life has begun.
The beginning of something new is there for you.

At the break of dawn, we see something new to unfold
For you at the break of dawn.

The time has come to go ahead, and do your thing
You would have it to be At the break of Dawn.

Life is fresh at the break of dawn. The dew has fallen on the grass
And the mist is in the air. The smell of flowers everywhere
At the break of dawn.

The mind is clear you can remember the day which is ahead
At the break of dawn.
The heavens unfold with all it's beauty for
you to witness and so your works
At the break of Dawn

~Lillie P. Gray~

Ministering in 1980's at Greater Community Temple COGIC
North Location, under Bishop W.L. Porter, Pastor and founder

THE GOD I SERVE

You my God is the one who made the world and everything in it. You are the Lord of heaven and earth, and you do not live in a temple built by hand. And you are not served by human hands you gave all men life and breath and everything else.

From one man you made every nation that they should inhabit the whole earth. You placed them everywhere to seek you. Ye shall walk after the Lord your God, and fear him, and keep his commandments, and obey his voice, and ye shall serve him, and cleave unto him Deut, 13:4. Wherefore we receiving a kingdom which cannot be moved, let us have grace, whereby we may serve God acceptably with reverence and godly fear. Hebrew 12:28. We must walk worthy of the calling of God who is Elohim our creator.

Great are you my Lord and most worthy of praise. One generation will tell of your mighty acts. My father heaven is your throne and the earth is your footstool (Isaiah 66:1). My lord you are slow to anger and great in power you will not leave the guilty unpunished, your way is in the whirlwind and the storm and the clouds are the dust of your feet (Nahum 1:3). My father and my God you are seated on a throne, high and exalted the train of your robe fills the temple above, you are calling to one another "Holy, holy, holy is the Lord hosts: the whole earth is full of his glory (Isaiah 6:1-3). Oh Lord, you are God. I will exalt you and praise your name, for in perfect faithfulness and truth you have done marvelous things planned long ago, (Isaiah 25:1). Now to the external immortal invisible, the only God, be honor and glory forever and ever. (1 Timothy 1:7)

RELEASING YOUR GIFTS

God's grace is with you to get you through whatever he is calling you to walk through. The key to releasing your gifts is to find the gifts God has for you. For example, Ephesians 4:11-12 states, "And he gave some apostles; and some prophets; and some evangelists; and some, pastors and teachers; for the perfecting of the saints, for the work of the ministry, for the edifying of the body of Christ". Start doing it then you will find grace and fulfillment that you have been looking for in your life. Paul also spoke about Robust peace is a forever force to disarm the devil. Peace is not external it is internal.

Peace is when you know your purpose and you know your vision and you are one with God on the issue you will not be moved from where God has called you to do. This is important because God anoints longevity when you stay in constant communication with him. You won't have a problem finding God, because you will be operating in the spiritual radar system of your gift and God will answer your call. For gifts and callings of God are without repentance (Rom. 11:29).

Satan will try to hinder what God has ordained in your life to complete your mission. You must tell the devil "NO", get thee behind me Satan I must do the will of my Father that sent me. It is great honor to witness God's anointing operating in his people break strongholds from Satan attacks. Releasing one's gifts takes the anointing of God and his approval in the spirit that he has given believers to be like him that he may be edified as well as gloried. We are his helpmate that he left here, to complete his work here on earth until he returns.

Take heed therefore unto yourselves, and to all the flock, over which the Holy Ghost hath made you overseers, to feed the church of which he hath purchased with his own blood" (Acts 20:28).

PROOF OF PURSUIT

God is not holding out on you. He wants to work miracles. Miracles in your life all around you. Jesus gave an example of a miracle in the prophet Jonah. He spent three days and nights in the belly of the big fish, so will the son of man spend three days and night in the depth of the earth. On the judgment day the people of Nineveh will stand up and accuse you because they turned from sins when they heard Jonah preach. (Mark 8:11; Luke 11:29-32) Manifestation is given to all who walk in your gift. The gifts and callings of God is without repentance. A spirit is given by the Holy Spirit according to God grace that the body might be effectual. Developed according to God's will.

There was a man sent from God his name was John, the same came for a witness to bear witness of the light that all men through him might believe. He was not that light, but was sent to bear witness of that light.

Each one has his or her limitation you can reach your goals no matter what they are. If you put your trust in the Lord! Him first, and you second you can achieve it. Don't limit yourself to anything, for God has already approved whatever you desire if you put him first in your life. No one can stop you from your goals in him.

We might have came from a poor family - but our heavenly father is rich. He make you a caretaker of the good fruit of the land and you reap the harvest of plenty. You don't have to want for anything it's there.

GOD'S ASSIGNMENT: WHERE DO YOU FIT IN HIS VINEYARD DOING HIS WORK

God has many offices in the church for his handmaids to complete the work he left on earth after two thousand years after his death. We must find what place do we complete the work he left undone. God choose people he can trust knowing everything about us, he's just waiting on us to make our move. If you ask yourself what shall I do that would be pleasing in the sight of God, knowing that all things work together for our good who is called according to his purpose.

We must search ourselves and be led by the spirit of God to know that it is God and we love him. Crucified the flesh and put on the whole armor of God to fight off the attack of the enemies for there are many who will seek to stop our purpose for the Lord.

Stay focus and anchored in the wisdom of God, who will lead you into all truth. No good thing shall He withhold from you who are called and ordained by him. Let every man abide in the same calling where he was called. (1 Cor. 7:20). God has his angels around us to protect us from many pitfalls and traps that Satan has laid for His children. Being a child of the King has many benefits all you have to do is give him a clean life and He shall use you and pure heart.

If you have a positive life you can't talk about your miserable past, change your attitude the words of our mouth will bring results, good or bad watch what you say. "Say what God say's" you come in agreement with God. For with the heart men believed unto righteousness and with the mouth confession is made unto salvation (Rom. 10:10).

WHAT DRIVES YOUR LIFE?

The basic motive for success is the driving force of envy and jealousy (Eccl. 4:4). The man without purpose is like a ship without a rudder a waiting a nothing a man (Thomas Carlyle). Everyone life is driven by something. The verb drive means to guide, to control, or to direct whether you are driving a car, a nail, or a golfball you are guiding, controlling and directing it that moment. What is the driving force in your life whether you are pressured by problems, a deadline, a painful memory, a hurting fear or an unconscious belief.

God there are many circumstance value and emotion that can drive your life. Many people are driven by guilt they spent their entire lives running from regrets and hiding their shame. Guilt driven people are manipulated by memories they allow their past to control their own success.

When Cain sinned his guilt disconnected him from the presence of God and God told Cain he would be a restless wonder on the earth (Genesis 4:16). Cain went out from the presence of the Lord, and dwelt in the land of Nod on the east of Eden. That's what some people are doing today, wandering through life without a purpose. We are products of our past, but we don't have to be prisoners' of it. Halleluiah.

God's purpose is not limited by our past, he turned Moses who was a murderer, into a leader and a coward named Gideon into a courageous hero, and he can do amazing things with the rest of your life. Praise God. You can be a winner, thanks be unto the all mighty God who all blessings flow. God specializes in giving people a fresh start, Hallelujah.

The Bible says what happiness for those whose guilt has been forgiven confessed their sins and God has cleared their record; Halleluiah.

Remember, he is helping a record. Praise God, bless His name when facing difficulties you don't have to dial 911, just call on the name of Jesus who is your present help in the time of trouble (Jere. 33:3). You have the telephone in your bosoms the heart which has received salvation through Jesus Christ God has given you power over Satan, to give you the victory.

BREAKING THE BARRIERS OF THE PAST

euteronomy 1:6 The Lord our God spake unto us in Ho-reb, saying, ye have dwelt long enough in this mount;
You have been where you are long enough to get a bigger perception of God. Don't let your past set the limit you are going, keep your mind on God.

Come up and come out, get in the center of Christ. Have you made a covenant with God? If so, God is holding you accountable for the things you have told him you would do. Your promise to God is a covenant, a contract you can't break. When you received salvation, that was a covenant with God to give his blessing of eternal life, and the riches here on earth.

Psalm 24:1 says, The earth is the Lord and the fullness thereof, the world and they that dwell there in.

You might have come from a poor family, but our heavenly father is rich. He makes us caretaker of the good fruit of the land and we reap the harvest of plenty. You don't have to want for anything, it all belong to him. Know that you are a joint heir of Jesus Christ.

Don't be like the children of Israel, always going back on their word to God, keep the faith and keep the covenant you made.

Matthew 9:17 Neither do men put new wine into old bottles; else the bottles break, and the wine runneth out, and the bottles perish; but they put new wine into new bottles, and both are preserved.

You can't put new wine in old wine skin, are you ready to change your thinking? Take the limit off God and your Life. Holiness has nothing to do with poverty. God is a God of abundance, don't think small. Enlarge your vision. Praise God. *Psalm 121:1-2 I will lift up mine eyes unto the hills, from whence cometh my help. My help cometh from the Lord which made heaven and earth.*

POWER OF WORD

on't sweat the small things that God give you. Go in your prayer closet and seek God for what you need. (THE SECRET PLACE OF THE MOST HIGH, PS91). Calling those things to be, not if they exist believe God for the impossible.

When you believe in your heart and confess with your mouth put the angles on the run to bring it to pass (Romans 10:10). God is a way maker a habit breaker. God will never fail, only you must believe.

God is the creator of heaven and earth and every physical thing seen and unseen. God is Satan boss he has authority over him (Luke 9:1). Your decisions molds your character and will determine what you will become, making better life decisions children will ask questions, you can look yourself in the mirror and know that you made the right decision. Don't take advice from just anybody don't listen to your friends, they will give you the wrong decision ask God for direction for your future destiny.

HANG ON IN THERE

he Lord bless thee, and keep thee (Num. 6:24). Faith comes by hearing and hearing by the word of God (Rom. 10:17). Faith has power to change things. If ye continue in the faith grounded and settled, and be not moved away from the hope of the gospel, which ye have heard, and which was preach to every creature which is under heaven; wherefore I Paul am made minister (Col. 1:23)

Deaf and life is in the power of the tongue watch what you speak. Love is a decision. Obey God what God told you to do you must be willing the love of God come as you are to God and he'll forgive and love you. I am reminded Ruth who was a Moabites. She married her son and Chili in Bethlehem of Judea, Elimelech, Naomi husband died and she was left with two sons. They took two wives, Orpah and Ruth. Both sons died and Naomi was left alone with her daughter in-laws. She wanted to return to her home in Bethlehem. And they lifted up their voice and wept again: Orpah kissed her mother-in-law; but Ruth clave unto her (Ruth 1:14).

Ruth hung on in there with her mother in-law and told her where I will lodge with you. She moved with her with her husband kinsman a family which was a mighty man of wealth the family Elimelech and his name was Boaz. Naomi named changed to Mara, Ruth meets Boaz and she receives favor from him. Her mother in-law gave her instruction how to carry herself in the fields with the servants that was set over the fields to glean for corn. She hanging on in there and she received a harvest and became Boaz with a wealth man. She stayed fast by the maiden of Boaz to glean unto the end of Barley harvest and wheat and carried it to her mother in-law. She hung on in there. There was victory when showed love for her mother in-law and led her into another face of her life to receive the victory because she hung on in there.

So hang on in there, let the Lord control your life and ye shall reap a great reward of his kingdom where we ceases to no problems everyday will be Sunday a day of jubilee to rejoice of our victory in Christ Jesus (Matt. 5:12). We must hang on in there and put all our trust in the Lord, for he will supply us with all our needs no matter how great or small they are. He is the answer to all our problems if we put our trust in the Lord. For he is our salvation, our straight, our strength reverence to whatever the problem might be. Hang on in there. Faith is the things hoped for and the evidence of things not seen (Rom. 8:28). There is no failure in God. There are times when our faith is tested to see how strong we are in the Lord **scripture** but we must hang on in there and depend on our help which comes from the Lord. For he is with us even until the end 1 Cor 1:9). God is faithful by whom ye were called unto the fellowship of his son Jesus Christ our Lord.

Seek ye first the kingdom of God and all others things shall be added unto you/ Life has many seen and unseen problems, but we can't give up we must meet our adversary with confidence that we can be over comers and allow problems if we put our trust in the Lord. Luke 18:1, and he spake a parable unto them to this end that men ought always pray and not faint.

The Lord will fullfill his promises to give us the desires of our heart, if only we put our total trust in Him and not waver. You can not serve God and man you must come all the way with the Lord in order to receive his total blessing. Don't be discourage when things go wrong for we must bear our cross the same as our Lord Jesus Christ before we can enter into the kingdom of God.

THERE IS JOY IN WAITING ON GOD

*P*salms 16:11 *Thou wilt show me the path of life; in thy presence is fullness of joy; at thy right hand there are pleasures for ever more.*

Jeremiah 15:16 Thy words were found, and I did eat them; and thy word was unto me the joy and rejoicing of mine heart; for I am called by the name, O Lord God of Host.

There are times when we become impatient for the Lord to answer our prayers and fulfill our needs. God will do only what you let him do -- If you wait on Him.

We are in the storms of life but God will bring you out of your storms. PRAISE THE LORD!!! HALLELUJAH

You will find joy if you wait on him. He holds the key in his hands for everything and he will unlock the door to meet your needs. Put your total trust in him and reap the benefits of his blessing.

Isaiah 40:31 He that waited upon the Lord shall renew their strength he shall mount upon wings like eagles in a nest. They shall run and not faint and not become weary.

"Teach us Lord How to Wait"

How many of us are willing to wait on the Lord. We must have patience to receive the blessing of God. Just wait on God he'll come where you need him. Just call him with your sincere heart and spirit of God that lives in you. Step back and let go and let God. He that waited upon the Lord shall renew their strength he shall mount upon wings like eagles in a nest they shall run and not faint and not become weary teach me Lord how to wait (Isa. 40:31;Ps 25:5

GOD COMMISION
CHRISTIAN WORKERS

ive us a watch word for the hour a thrilling word of power a battle cry a flaming breath a call to conquest or to death. A work to rouse the church from rest to heed the master on high. The call is give ye host the watchword is *"evangelize, excuse not now"*. Every time you say no is more difficult to say yes. The time and the day is not "behold, now is the accepted time. Behold, now I the day of salvation; 1 Chron. 16;23 seek the Lord while he may be found delay his decision for the wrong way. Today if you will saith the Lord. Tomorrow is the day when the idle man work the thief become honest the drunkard sober, tomorrow is a period no where to be found except perhaps in the fool calendars.

God call is not a call for tomorrow but for today. Jesus came and spoke unto them, saying all power is given unto me in Heaven and in earth. Go ye therfor, and teach all nations, baptizing them in the name of the father, son, and the holy ghost, teaching them to observe all things whosoever I have commanded you; and lo, I am with you always, even unto the end of the world (Matt. 28:18-20). O' son of man I have set thee a watchman, therefore thou shalt hear the word of my mouth, and warn them for me, I thou doest speak to the wicked man shall die in his iniquities but his blood will I require at thou hand (Ezek. 33:18); God is looking to us to evangelize tell about his goodness and he'll do everything for you in your time of need. God and spread the word that God has come to serve the world. Let the work of Christ dwell in you richly in all wisdom; teaching and admonishing one another in psalms and hymns and spiritual songs, singing with grace in your hearts to the Lord (Col. 3:16).

CHURCH "BODY OF CHRISTIANS"

As we become a saint of God we become a witness to carry the good news about our Jesus Christ. Praising God and having favor with all people and the Lord added to the church daily such as should be saved (Acts 2:47). God is looking for a church, He is looking at our faithfulness to serve Him. He's looking for somebody that will humble themselves unto Him. Put all not some but all their trust in him. He is looking for a church that we can help build (which is the body of Christ) "praise God" not man made church that's not what he is looking for, we have a lot of work to do in building this church. Helping sinners men, boys, and girls find this church the one God has made for as to enter into his Kingdom that heavenly home with him eternal home our souls through salvation.

ALL THAT I AM AND
ALL I HOPE TO BE

All that I am and all I hope to be, free as a
bird in a tree singing a melody
It's sweet to hear a tune you want to be.
We see the wind blowing swiftly through the trees, we
are hoping to be all that we can and want to be.
We measure our steps as we trail along
Trying to make it to our heavenly home,
We must be all that we are and want to be
To receive the blessing that awaits us there.

I hope to win a trophy of God to bless me there
Because I am what He wants me to be.

Lillie P. Gray 7/4/2001

Don't Surrender Leadership to Frustration and Fear

(Leaders must Pray)

Proverbs 11:30 The fruit of the righteous is a tree of life; and he that winneth souls is wise.

Leaders must have a prayer life in order to lead others to Christ Jesus. All that we do and says must be led by the spirit of God. We must have the anointing of God and the Word of God on the inside of us so that God's people will be led into all truth. Without that we can't be good leader.

Ephesians 6: 18 Praying always with all prayer and supplication in the Spirit, and watching thereunto with all perseverance and supplication for all saints; Leaders are to always pray, so that God's people will be blessed with a right now Word from on high to minister to their needs, circumstances and concerns. So when the enemy tries to stop or hinder you from going to the throne of grace to pertition God on others behalf, or your ministry don't get frustrated, don't surrender your leadership, don't throw in the towel and don't give in just continue to call on the name of the Lord and he will deliver.

A praying leader will show love, patience, toleration, temperance in all things, faith and endurance. Prayer brings God's will to pass and moves him into action, he acts on your behalf.

Don't Surrender Leadership to Frustration and Fear

(Leaders must Pray)

Great Leaders faces great challenges, and many of the greatest pioneers in the church were forced to become "great repenters". This is necessary when you make up your mind to live holy before God.

God is still on the throne, we're His footstool, and there is only knee distance between us. Leaders PRAY, PRAY and PRAY.

1ˢᵗ Thessalonians 5:17 Pray without ceasing

"DON'T LET YOUR AGE STOP YOU, IT'S ONLY A NUMBER"

Whatever you purpose in your mind to perceive it and you can achieve it. Stop and listen to your inner "thought process" and seek guidance from your heavenly father which is your source to bring anything to pass. But seek ye the kingdom of God, and his righteousness; and all these things shall be added unto you (Matt. 6:33). Nothing is too small or large, he will handle it and give you direction. A mind is terrible thing to waste. Think on those things to become possible for all things to come to pass. A mind is a terrible thing to waste. You have mind cells that has not been used, open them up to the impossible and "think" and you can achieve. You must have a goal. Set time for completion. God responds to faith, learn how to walk in the will of God. For we walk by faith and not by sight (2 Cor. 5:7). With all your getting it must be the wisdom of God . But without faith it is impossible to please him; for he that cometh to God must believe that he is and a rewarder of them that diligently seek him (Heb. 11:6).

HEED THE CALL

Your righteousness in God (Genesis 1:26)

You were made in the image of God. You know God is a spirit and you are a spirit the outer garment is the shell that up live in, but the spirit of God is just like him.

We are going to realize that we are not living in the fullness of God. We are just like him a spirit that made us into his own image and he breathed his spirit into us.

We are living beneath our privileges as heirs of God and his kingdom if we don't claim who we are in Christ Jesus.

This outer body will decay but the spirit of God will never die. He placed us here to complete his work here on earth if we are in Christ Jesus who is our savior. God sent his own begotten son into the world that we might be saved for our sins (John 3:16-19).

A person who is not walking in the light of God is in darkness. But if he believes and take on the image of God and receive salvation then he can walk into everlasting life in Christ Jesus. After receiving salvation God has called everyone to complete the work and not lean on his own understanding. Jesus tells his disciples in Matthew 6:33, to seek the knowledge of God and his righteousness and all things shall be added unto thee. He wants you to love him with sincere heart. Because you are a chosen vessel, a royal priesthood , a holy nation, a peculiar people that show forth praise unto him that has called you out of the darkness into the marvelous light (1 Peter 1:9). We want to be an image of our Father and be a giver of good gifts like God.

The worlds were framed by the word of God (Heb 11:3). Without words there would not have been any creation. Your words create images and eventually you will live out the reality of that image.

Every time you speak your faith it creates a stronger image inside you. It is healing you desire: the healing image is created by God's word and your continual affirmation and agreement with it. Eventually that image will be perfected by the word of God and will begin to see yourself well. When the word is engrafted into you it infuses its life into you (John 1:1-14).

A FATHER WHO CARES

*J*ehovah my God the one who formed the earth, mountains, creates the wind and rain, reveal his thoughts to man. He declared unto man what is his thoughts, that maketh the morning darkness, and treadeth upon the high places of the earth …(Amos 4:13).

This is what the Lord our God who formed places and made the heavens and earth. He hath established it, he created it not to be empty but formed it to be inhabited. I am the Lord, and there is none else (Isa. 45:18).

We as the children of God, we must walk in his statue and be worthy of the calling that he placed on your life. God will use you if you make yourself available to him. God Almighty Lord, I acknowledge that you are the "I am" this is your name by which you are to be remembered from generation to generation (Exodus 3:14-15).

My father helps me to know that the Lord my God is God. You are faithful, you have kept your covenant of love to a thousand generations of those who you love and keep your commands (Deut. 7:9). God you are my rock, your works are perfect and all your ways are just and you are faithful and just (Deut. 34:4). You my father are my loving God and my fortress; my stronghold, and my deliverer, my shield in whom I take refuge, who subdues people under me (Ps. 144:2).

WE MUST WORK WHILE IT IS DAY

God is looking for a people that he can use. We are the vessels that he has to depend on, the body of Christ. We are to carry out the mission that he has set before us here on earth. One of these days we will give an account of our stewardship. God placed us here to do his work. I have made you servant over many. How many did we tell that God was real? You live and trust him while it is day. God is taking record of everything we do. We made him a promise we would be his helper, we'll be his hands, his mouth, his feet. He give us his thought. How many of us today have kept our vows we made with the God? We made a covenant that we must keep.

Women of God when we made a vow with our husband, that was before God. We must obey that vow. We don't know what's ahead of us, but God said through good times, bad times, sick and health we must keep that vow we made. God is holding you to that vow.

God will help you through every step of the way. I know what it means to do what God has given us to do. My husband was sick for five years. It wasn't easy. Three strokes, a broke hip, and eye surgery to remove cataracts because he was going blind. He was not easy to deal with, but God gave me strength to go through. It became rough and I asked God, " how long must I go through?" And He said, "I will exalt you in due time." Our timing is not God's timing. "Low I am with you even until the end . You hold on and I will reward you for your faithfulness. I will bless your going and coming, there shall be no lack in your life. I shall multiply your seed, your children children's shall be blessed just keep my commandments and victory is yours says the Lord."

Prayer Changes Things

How many of us know that God will answer prayer? Have we tried him for yourself? Have we put our total trust in him and know that he will bring you out of any situation. If you trust him all you got to do is go into your prayer closet and ask what you will of the savior and he'll give you the victory and bring you out. Nothing is too hard for God to solve, when you give it to Him. Humble yourself unto him and put your total trust in Him.

A TRAIN RIDE TO GLORY

1979

**This train will make all stops to reach His Glory - Heaven Bound
1 Kings 10:2**

This train doesn't have a conductor, Jesus Christ is the conductor of this train, *Numbers 22:6* says, "That I may drive them out of the land: for I know that he whom is blesses is blessed, and he whom is cursed is cursed." Salvation can be received on this train. Healing can be received on this train. Faith is on this train. Everlasting peace is on this train. Get on board. **Jesus is calling!** Get on board. **Jesus is calling**! Because he is the conductor of this train. According to *Matthew 11:28*, Jesus says, "Come unto me all ye that labour and are heavy laden, and I will give you rest." Just listen for your name, he wants you to get on board. You can received holiness on this train you can receive justice on this train. He's making his stops, why don't you get on board.

He's stopping to get sinners on every corner. "**Flag this train down**!" Don't let him leave you behind. He's waiting to save you before it's too late. Then will I teach transgressors thy ways: and sinners shall be converted unto thee, *Psalm 51:13*. Cast all your cares upon him for he cares for you. He's waiting to pick you up and place your feet on solid ground. We are heaven bound on this train, we stand on holy ground !

He's never too full on this train. He's looking for you to go everywhere in Him which is the Spirit Of God that is given to you with love. "But God commend his love, toward us in that, *__while we were yet sinners Christ died for us.__ Much more then, being now justified by his blood, we* *shall be saved from wrath through him*. Roman 5:8-9. It don't matter what the problem he can solve them. Liars, cheaters, whoremongers, gamblers, thieves and robbers, murders, adultery, idolatry, homosexuals, hatred, and drunkenness …..that which do such things will not inherit the kingdom of God. But the fruit of the Spirit is love, joy, peace, longsuffering, gentleness, goodness, faith, meekness, temperance: against such there is no law, Galatians 5:8-23. God will forgive, and wants you to get onboard.

He's stopping by to pick you up. Call on him at every stop. Get on board. Don't make no excuse- He's a just God. Don't let the devil trick you any longer. He's a deceiver. Tell him to get back Satan. **I'm getting off to catch the Train to Glory**. I am **laying down my sins and taking Jesus for he can save me**. I have had enough, "Devil !!" I realize that God is my source. I am not ashamed of the Gospel. I will be an overcomer through Christ Jesus, (Romans 1:16). Praise God from whom all blessing flow. He is worthy of the praise.

God will reach down inside of you and deliver you from bondage and the Holy Spirit will dwell within you because Satan is forever present to take your mind into his realm of sin. Stay focused on what God has done for you. My people shall not have no shame of what they went through.

"Awake , ye drunkards, and weep; and howl,…" (Joel 1:5). Let us lay aside every weight and sin that so easily best us…(Hebrew 12:1).

Stay strong in the Lord, read his word daily---you must have the Holy Ghost which is that keeping power. Acts 2:1,4 says, "And when the day of Pentecost was fully come, they were all with one accord in one place… And they were filled with the Holy Ghost, and began to speak with other tongues, as the Spirit gave them utterance". That is what happens when you board this train. All your habits was taken captive and you became new in Christ Jesus through salvation. On this train God did it and we are glad about it. Praise God !!! I will bless the Lord at all times and his praises shall continue be in my mouth (Psalm 34:1). The things you use to do there is no desire for you to return. We must stay on board of this Train to Glory to receive eternal life in Christ Jesus. To live in abomination of sin prepares you to join your guest in the pit of hell. *"And there shall in no wise enter into it any thing that defileth, neither whatsoever worketh abomination, or maketh a lie: but they which are written in the Lamb's book of life"* (Revelation 21:27).

You must live so that God can use you anywhere, anytime. Let the Spirit of God flow in and out of you and sinners will know that you are a child of the King. You have became a light on this train. The Spirit of

God is shining through you so that you can reach other sinners when this train makes it stop to get them on board. Praise God !!!

God will use you when you become available to His Holy Spirit because he knows you have taken on the Spirit of him to help sinners to believe in him. But in the multitude of counsel there is safety to become a teacher of the word . "The fruit of righteousness is a tree of life; and he that winneth souls is wise" (Proverbs 11:30). Praise God, Praise God, we thank him for all things.

WOMAN ANOINTED FOR THE KINGDOM

(Esther Prepared To Save Her People)

Prayer

My Father heaven is your throne and the earth is your footstool. My Lord you are slow to anger and great in power. You will not leave the guilty unpunished. Your way is in the whirlwind and the storm, and clouds are the dusk of your feet.

O Lord you are my God, I will exalt you and praise your name for in perfect faithfulness you have done marvelous things planned long ago. Now to the King eternal, mortal, invisible, the only God be honor and glory for ever and ever.

We ask your blessing upon us tonight, bless our effort to please you and no flesh glory in your sight. May I decrease that you may increase in the Holy Spirit have his way in me. Word these lips of clay, let your perfect will be done. Amen

The Book Of Esther is the last book of history as prescribed. It tells of the victory of God special people who were doomed to die although the name of God is not to be found anywhere within this book, there is every indication that he is working on behalf of his special people of that day.

The book of Esther, is said to be during the end of the Persian Rule and the beginning of the March of Alexander the Great wherein the welfare of Israel was invalid. Esther won the contest of beauty and became the Queen of Persia, which became an advantage toward the freedom of the Jews who were otherwise doomed to die.

The book of Esther is noted to have the longest verse in the Bible, Esther 8:9. The content of the book justifies the Jewish feast known as "The Feast Of Purim" which commemorates the events that inspired as narrated within the book of Esther.

Esther 1:1-3

1. Now it came to pass in the days of A-has-u-e-rus, (this is A-has-u-e`rus

which reigned, from India even unto E-thi-o-pi-a, *over* and seven and twenty provinces:)

2. *That* in those days, when the king A-has-u-e`rus sat on the throne of his kingdom, which was in Shu`shan the palace.

3. In the third year of his reign, he made a feast unto all his princes and his servants; the power of Per`sia and Me`di-a, the nobles and princes of the provinces, *being* before him:

They had a feast and was draped in their riches. They had fine line, and purple to silver rings and pillows of marble. The beds were of gold and silver and white and black marble..

They were rich in wealth of all things that the King needed to live in his palace. They gave them drink in vessels of gold. The vessel was diverse one from another and royal wine in abundance according to the state of the King.

They were appointed to do what ever was the King pleasure---
That what we do in our lives according to what please the flesh.

Mordecai sat at the gate and watched Esther carry out the plan to free their

people the "Jews". He was able to reveal to Esther the plan that Haman to betray the King. Esther was able to tell the King of his betrayal. The King ordered Mordecai to enter his palace. He was robed in fine garments and a ring was placed on his finger from the King and he gave Queen Esther Haman's house and set over Haman's house, Esther 8:2,7. The plan failed for Haman. He was hanged on the very same gallows that he intended for Mordecai.

Romans 12:16b

Mind not the high things, condescend to men of low estate. Be not wise in your conceits. This is how the Lord bring things to pass in front of your enemies. Scripture says the God will make your enemy your footstool. Praise God for the battle is not ours but the Lord God Almighty.

The anointing that came upon her was that of FAVOR and was the kind that cause her to wave her hand and speak a word and something marvelous happen but it came housed in the package of favor.

In Esther 8:5, Esther says, " If I have found favour in his sight, and the thing seem right before the king, and being pleasing in his eyes, let it be written…

So the King granted Esther request. The anointing is not just to run around the church. God has a plan to use you as his vessel to complete the mission before you. Proverbs 21:1 - The king's heart is in the hand of the LORD, as the rivers of water: he turneth it whithersoever the will.

Conclusion:

WHAT CAN WE LEARN FROM THE STORY OF QUEEN ESTHER?

1. God will turn you into the direction that he need to use you. God had already set it up: If God is with and for us --- no weapon directed against us can succeed. But, God works in mysterious ways. Esther was the daughter of Ab-ihail who died earlier and Mordecai Esther uncle by marriage, took Esther into his home and brought her up as his own daughter. He dearly loved her (Esther 2:15). Because of Esther great beauty she was notice by the King at the hour he was replacing queen Vashti, who had refused the King's invitation to parade her beauty before his drunken guest Esther 1:12. **Vashti name means once desired**.

That is when Mordecai told Esther that the LORD has saved her for "Such a time as this" Esther 4:14). Esther name means "Star". Esther 2:17 says, "the King loved Esther above all women, she obtained grace and favor in his sight more than all the virgins: so that he sat the royal crown upon her head instead of Vashti".

2. In spite of all the trials and tribulations that will occur in our lives we must stay focus in Jesus Christ who is the author and finisher of our faith. He knows just what we need. We must be steadfast, unmovable knowing that GOD still has control and he will make a way of escape for us to come out victorious in our lives.

Regardless what the problem is he is Alpha and Omega, the First and Last. He is Elohim the creator, Jehovah-Jireh our provider. He is Jevoah-Roah, the LORD is my Shepherd. A GOD for all times, all places, all needs. "The same yesterday, today, and forever". Praise God from whom all blessing flow. Amen.

HOLINESS IS THE ANSWER

God gave his life that we might be saved. We as Christian have been chosen by God with his divine spirit to carry the good news about him. We must live holy in order to do things for God who sent his only son Christ Jesus into all the world that we might be saved.

Without him we are nothing. We must be holy no matter what the price you have to pay. God paid it all. To him we owe. Praise God. Praise God. We must set an example in our life to live where God can use us anywhere and anytime we must think holiness, walk holy, look holy. We should live holy separated from all unrighteousness where the world, men, women, and children may see our good works in Christ Jesus.

Declare his glory among the heathen; his marvelous work among all nations for great is the Lord and greatly to be praised. He's also to be feared above all. Glory and honor in his presence. Strength and gladness in his place.

Give unto the Lord ye kindred's of the people. Give unto the Lord Glory and strength.

We are following the works of God going about doing good to all people. No matter what or where we are holy women of God. Praise God. God has no respect of person we are all God people he's looking for a people that will live for him and do his perfect will.

We as women of God have a responsibility. We must be God fearing women, we are a vital part of the spiritual nation. We have to be a role model for others to follow from the cradle to the grave.

Holiness is when times get hard, and yet you trust God, because you know he can deliver you, there is no failure in God. God will give you power over the devil. You can remain holy. Holiness is not what you wear-where you live, how much money you have. Who you know. Holiness is when we realize that GOD is the upmost in your lives. God is Alpha and Omega, the beginning and the end. He is our total source.

He's taking note of our life each and every day. Our record is recorded each and everyday in the lamb book of life. God will help his promise. But we must keep his commandments. The word of God is our road map to receive our just reward which is in him.

You must live a holy life without a spot or wrinkle of unholiness, and he will show up in your life. He will manifest himself. Ye shall be blessed. God so a right now. God he holds the world in his hands. He is the great "I AM".

We as saints of God must be strong in his word for we will be tempted by things of the world. But we must know when to say 'no" to the things that are not of God. When you live close to God he'll lead you in his statue. His perfect will. We can not get caught up in little clicks in the church. The wrong Amen Corner. Some that are wearing sheep's clothing, you know what I mean. The ones straddle the fence, foolers in the church. We must ask God to give us a spiritual eye, a discernment of the spirit to know them. When we get down to it. When you are trying to live holy, the devil gets busy. **Watch out!** Praise God. Don't give him any room in your life. Stay focused on things of God and they will flee from you. When God show up the devil can't stay. He will have to go. Praise God. Praise God.

I am reminded of Miriam both her words and her works were full of inspiration of God. She was gifted poetess and prophetess's a leader and a pattern to women of Israel prophets and prophetess are raised up by God and inspirited by his spirit to proclaim the will and purpose of God (Exodus 15:20).

If we had the opportunity to save someone could we be like Miriam who was only ten or twelve years old when she saved her brother who Moses. God gave her wisdom because he knew he had plans for Moses life (Exodus 2:7).

Women, God used Abraham and he can use us; we are the seed of Abraham, a chosen generation, a blessed people and heirs of his kingdom. Wake up and see the salvation of the Lord. *Look* up your help comes from God. *Reach* out and he will lead you in path of righteousness for his sake for ever and ever. Praise God. Praise God.

Bless his holy name. Who wouldn't serve a God like that. Bless his holy name. Bless him. Hallelujah

I can remember in my life I had to make a chose between what was best for me. I am so glad that I choose to stay on the Lord side. I been in the valley, but God picked me up, and placed my feet on higher ground. I been through the fire in this church, he gave me a spirit of holiness and I am glad about it. Praise God.

H - Holy Women are Honest I Peter 2:12
O - Holy Women are Obedient I Peter 1:14-15
L - Holy Women are the Light: Let their light shine so men may see there good works
I - Holy Women are Intercessor when you need to get a prayer through.
N - Holy Women are Needful James 2:16
E - Holy Women are an Example I Tim 4:12
S - Holy Women are Submissive Ephesians 5:22
S - Holy Women are Saints Romans 1:7

In my conclusion:

"Women of the Lord" Holy Women Blood brought dedicated woman, consecrated women;

Arise, Shake thou self from the dust, the dust of the mind, complacency and confusion.

Awake, Awake. Put on strength. Strength the weak hand. Conform the feeble knee. Lift up your head and hands and praise him.

We have responsibility Holy Women, we must face it. We can not except it. Let your works praise ye into the gates. Praise God - Praise

GOD WILL KEEP HIS PROMISE

The promise of Isaac birth(Genesis 15:1)

V 15 And the Lord said unto Abraham as for Sari thy wife, thou shalt not call her name Sari, but Sarah shall her name be.

V16 And I will bless her and give thee a son also of her: yea I will bless her, and she shall be a mother of nations: kings of people shall be of her.

V17 Then Abraham fell upon his face and laughed, and said in his heart, shall a child be born unto him that is a hundred years old? And shall Sarah, that is ninety years old hear?

V19 And God said, Sarah thy wife shall bear thee a son indeed, and thou shall call his name Isaac, and I will establish my covenant with him for an everlasting covenant, and with his seed after him.

Abraham's Name Change

Genesis 17

V5 Neither shall thy name anymore be called Abram but thy name shall be Abraham, for a father of many nations have I made thee.

V6 And I will make thee exceeding fruitful, and I will make nations of thee, and kings shall come out of thee.

V7 and I will establish my covenant between me and thee and thou seed after thee in their generations for an everlasting covenant, to be a God unto thee, the land wherein thou a stranger, all the land of Cannan, for an everlasting possession and I will be thou God.

Hagar is the first surrogate mother. Sara decided to share her husband with Hagar because she was barren. Haggar was given all kinds of good treatment from Abraham.

Sara endured this because she thought that God wasn't going to bless her in her late years because she was seventy and Abraham was 100 years old. Hagar gave birth to a son his name was Ishmael. Sara became jealous and told Abraham they had to leave. She realize that God had told her he would bless her womb and she would give birth to a son - she doubted God and his promise.

God don't lie, whatever he promise he will deliver. It shall come to pass. You must wait on him. Your timing is not God's timing. He will keep his promise. He will give you the victory in all your ways if you trust him. Don't let the devil fool you. Keep your mind on God.

A miracle is about to happen. God blessed Sara when the odds was against her and Abraham. He gave her a son. His name was Isaac. Isaac and Ishmael grew up together. ***The Miracle (Isaac) and The Mistake (Ishmael). The wheat and the tare.*** If you don't deal with your failure you will deal with your mistake. You must get tried yourself and make a change. Sara had prayed for this miracle (Gen. 18:14), Is anything to hard for the Lord? Sara told Abraham to put Haggar out of the tent, it was easy for Sara to tell Haggar to go. Haggar had dreams hoping as a kept woman it would last. It wasn't easy for Abraham to put Haggar out. He had become bound to Haggar. She said I know you love Ishmael, but you must put her away. Praise God.

God had a blessing for Abraham. He obeyed God and put them out. Praise God. God want you to give up the things you love for him, put him above all. Whatever the situation might be, God will give you strength to go through. Praise God.

Somewhere in your life you have left something that was a sacrifice for God. You don't know what I been through, but God will bring you out, you must give God the praise through it all. Praise God. God will give you the victory. Give God the Glory. It's your time and your season. You plant your seed in good soil and now it germinated and your harvest is plenty. Praise God.

Believe in yourself - be effective. You are never to old to make your dream come true. As for me, a late bloomer, God did it for me -bless my life - gave me victory. Believe in the impossible it shall become possible if you believe in God. He will make it come to pass through your faith.

You ask and it shall be given unto you put the devil under your feet. Call a;; things of God promises and believe and receive it. Make the devil a lie - put him under your feet and out of your life. Believe God.

Meditate on the word day and night. God said ye shall prosper and be in good health even as your soul prosper. Which mean your total being. Praise God.

Develop you faith by staying in the word of God. Praise God.

Don't be jealous of somebody who is blessed of the Lord. Praise God.

Use the same weapon the word of God that is your sword to divide the word of truth to reach your destiny in life. Praise God. God is your source.

Start speaking your freedom, your mouth is connecting to things that has to be spoken to speak it into action. Speak to that mountain. Tell it to get out of your way.

You need to have your children in the word with you. You must build your house on the Rock which is Jesus the word of God. I have to spend time in the word you must have a plan.

When they went into the promise land they were attacked by Bales. He is the devil. The Lord wants to be Lord over your children. We don't tell our children about the good we need to show them how to live by the word of God. God will raise up people who will not comprise keep standing. Hang in there. Look the devil in the eye and tell him you are going to win - you will conquer him. Bales loosing and God winning. We take a strong stand Bale is a evil spirit. We must stand not for garbage of this day. When you are healed now when you see your finance increased.

Create an open heaven of faith you must tithe. You can't be a thief robbing God. You must be a giver not a taker Isa. 4:18. I will open rivers in high places, and fountains in the midst of the valleys. I will make the wilderness a pool of water and the dry land springs of water. I have raised him up in righteousness and I will direct al his ways he shall build my city, and he shall let go my captives, not for price nor reward said the Lord of host (Isa. 45:15). And even to your old age I am he and to hoar hairs will I carry you and I will deliver you (Isa 46:4). Return ye backsliding children, and I will heal, you backsliding, behold, we come unto thee for thou art the Lord our God (Jer. 3:22).

IF THEY CAN'T RULE
THEY TRY TO RUIN YOU

*Y*our perception determines who you are in Christ Jesus. We must have a spiritual ear to hear and know which direction God is guiding us in our daily walk with Christ Jesus.

Be strong in the Lord and let go and God will manifest those gifts that he has given you.

Hold your head up and stick your chest out and believe God and say, "Yes I can." He can bring forth Holy Ghost power in you. And I am sure that God, who began the good work within you, will continue his work until it is finally finished on that day when Christ Jesus comes back again (Philippians 1:6 NLT).

You are a child of the king, the most high God. Elohim our creator. Our DNA can be tested with a swipe of a swab in our mouth to determine if we are related. But to determine if we are related to Jesus Christ God will test us to see if we are spirit filled. We must obtain salvation through repentance of our sins and confess with our mouth that Jesus Christ is Lord (Romans 3:23).

When God gives you an idea man will try to take credit and destroy your thought process. Jealously will prevail because man deceitful, cunning, conniving, and misleading to cause you to ruin Gods plan concerning you. But Jesus said in Matthew 21:42, "The stone which the builders rejected, the same is become the head of the corner: this is the Lord's doing and it marvelous in our eyes? You must be careful and listen to Christ Jesus for his direction to finish because he will always lead you in the right direction. Man will try to rule and ruin your reputation just like Potiphar's wife tried to ruin Joseph while he was Prime Minister over Egypt before the entire

Jewish nation and the people of the land (Genesis 39-49). God had a plan when Joseph brother's threw him in the pit. He was bought by a company of Ishmaelite, his cousin which had the same DNA.

Even though his brothers meant him evil, but God meant it for good. God had a plan for Joseph's life. Out all the things he went through Joseph when he was an anointed dreamer, which was a gift God gave him. He dreamed that his brothers and family would bow down to him when he was seventeen years old and they threw him in a pit.

When he was in prison, there was a butler and a baker who offend their lord the King of Egypt and Pharaoh threw them in prison. Both men dreams saddened them. The next morning Joseph saw them and asked them what was the matter. Both of them told him their dream. The butler dream was a about a vine and branches. Joseph interrupted Pharaoh will restore thee unto thy place and you shall serve Pharaoh as before. The baker's three white baskets on his head with birds eating from it. Joseph interrupted their dreams. He told the baker in three basket represent three days and Pharaoh shall lift up thee head off thee and shall hang thee on a tree and the birds shall the flesh off thee. And it came to pass. Gen 40:5.

The butler remembered Joseph when Pharaoh was searching the land of Egypt for someone to interpret his dream. Pharaoh summoned Joseph to king's court and ask Joseph if he could interrupt his dream about stand on the bank of the river, seven fat kine, seven poor very ill favored kine and the ill favor ate up the fatted kine. Joseph did not Immediately tell Pharaoh what his dream meant. The second part of the dream was' behold seven ears came up and one stalk, full and good, and behold seven ears withered thin and blasted with the east wind sprung up after them. And the thin ears devoured the seven good ears.

Gen. 41:26 The seven good kine are seven years; and the seven good ears are seven years: the dream is one. The just of the matter is that there will be seven good years and seven years of famine. Joseph suggested to Pharaoh that he look out a man discreet and wise, and set him over the land of Egypt and let him appoint officers over the land , and take up the fifth part of the land of Egypt in the seven plenteous years. Let them gather all the food of those good years that food may be stores in the land for the seven years of famine. Joseph reward was Pharaoh appointed him over the entire land of Egypt even his household and change his name to Zaphnathpaaneah and gave him a wife when he was thirty years old. Because the famine reached as far as Canaan where his father, brothers, and all seventy -five of family members had to leave Canaan and go down to Egypt. Not knowing that Joseph was ruler over Egypt. Joseph had much favor even though the Egyptian tried to ruin Pharaoh's decision to give the Israelites the land of Goshen to raise their stock. But God prevailed and they received favor. That tells you when people try to ruin you God's plan must be carried out no matter how many obstacles and pitfalls may come your way God is still in control. The End of that matter. Now do you believe in your God.

He is not only my rock and my salvation: he is my defense and I shall not be moved (Psalm 62:6).

LIVING IN THE
FULLNESS EVERYDAY

an't nobody change it nor amend it when his children cry. He lifted me out of a horrible pit and places my feet on solid ground… (Psalm 40:2). God alone can turn your life around. God gets the glory. Be healed and be set free. God is able to supply all your needs and I am free. "But my God shall supply all your need according to his riches in glory by Christ Jesus (Phil. 4:19)". Don't let Satan hinder your blessing in the Lord, Satan comes to you at all angles in your life. "For thou rock is as not as our Rock, even our enemies themselves being judges (Deut. 32:31). You must know how to shun evil and no that God is your everything everyday.

Things may get rough but that's when you can go to the Rock and that rock is Jesus. "He is the ROCK, his work is perfect: for all his ways are judgments: a God of truth and without iniquity, just and right is he (Deut. 32:4)". Scripture tell us "…If any man be in Christ, he is a new creature old things are passed away; behold, all things are become new (2 Cor 5:17)". He will turn it around and set you free. When your life get rough , you must fall down on your knees and pray. Father, I stretch my hand to thee. He will heal your land. Call him when you are in trouble. Call him when there is no money in bank and he will make a way. When you are sick call him. He's a healer. He's there ready to answer. Jesus is a right now God, ready and able to meet every need. All praises belong to God.

KNOWING THE FATHER'S VOICE

God choose all kind of ways to speak to his children. Beside using scripture directly, he uses our own inner desires, circumstances and the words and encouragement of others. The key for us is to pay attention and discerned what he is saying to us through those things.

When God spoke to him, he kept bringing him back to one scripture verse "My Sheep hear my voice and I know them and they follow me" (John 10:27), he saying, my sheep- those who have a relationship with me- hear my voice because they know me. They know my voice because it is distinguished from all others voices.

Remember, all kinds voices can get our attention, voices from within us, voices from the world around us. How do we know when it's God's voice speaking and not just our own desires or our circumstance? We know his voice because we know him. There is still small voices that will confirm his word in your heart. You should take the time to get to know your fathers voice. God speaks to us in many ways, when we get to know him.

My sheep know my voice and a stranger he will not follow. Follow after Christ. Let him lead and guide you into all truth.

DO SOMETHING
ABOUT WHAT YOU SEE

is mother was quite a housekeeper, she wanted thing tidy and in order and she worked hard to keep it that way. His mom didn't have a bit of a problem making sure his sisters and he did there share to keep things clean. She said " Boy, why don't you do something about what you see?

The Apostle James has plenty to say about "Do something about what you see", when it comes to the word of God.

James 1: 22-25 - *But prove yourselves doers of the word, and not merely hearers only, deceiving your own selves. For if any man be a hearer of the word, and not a doer, he is like unto a man beholding his natural face in a glass(mirror): For (once)he behold(looked at) himself, and goeth his way(gone his way), and straightway fretted(immediately forgotten) what manner(kind) of man he was. But whoso looked into the perfect law of liberty, and continueth therein, he being not a forgetful hearer, but a(effectual) doer of the work, this man shall be blessed in his deed.*

He stated that we can sit in the pews on Sunday morning and hear the word of God preached, go to our bible studies and even read the word for ourselves; but if we don't apply(live) what we hear or read than we are wasting our time (it's in vain).

There is incredible life-changing power in the word of God. James placed the scriptures to a mirror, we can look in to get an accurate picture of what we are really like, but when we can take a look at that picture and find out what needs to be changed, we can see and acknowledge that change is needed and through the power of the Holy Spirit make those changes.

When we do that, James tells us we will be blessed in all we do. On the other hand James point out, "we can be like a man who wakes up in the morning and looks at himself in the mirror." In order to do something about what you see, a change has to take place.

Roman 12: 1-2 I beseech you therefore, brethren, by the mercies of God, that you present you bodies a living sacrifice, holy, acceptable unto God, which is your reasonable service. And be not conformed to this world; but be ye transformed by the renewing of your mind, that ye may prove what is that good, and acceptable, and perfect, will of God.

God word is powerful, but remember it want do you any good until you purpose in your heart to apply it to your life.

We will have a victorious walk with Christ when we make sure that our faith is in him and not in leaders or organization. The Word of God states, *he will never leave us nor forsake you.*

Remember, Do something about what you see.

DON'T BE LED BY YOUR 5 SENSES

*P*roverbs 3:5-6 Trust in the LORD with all thine heart and lean not unto thine own understanding. "In all thy ways acknowledge him and he shall direct thy paths. (Proverbs 3:6)"

Your natural senses can be a hindrance in seeing and knowing who God really is. We tend to trust in our abilities and accomplishment and not trusting in God to handle everything in our life.

There will be times when you are in Church, seeing all the bad things, having focus on all the other stuff that goes on in the church. This sight can drive you from church, from fellowship and eventually from God. But if you keep your sight focused on God, you want have time to worry about what's going on in the church, what sister or brother so and so is doing, but your eyes will be focused on God, and how I need him to be the more. For it's in him(Christ) that I Live, Move and have by being. Can't do nothing without him, but with him you can do all things.

When you see God in the beauty of holiness, you are now seeing out your spiritual eyes and everything in life, every circumstance, every situation you will be able to see Christ.

Hearing requires silence sometimes or being alone - He that hath an ear to hear, let him hear what the spirit of the Lord is saying.

Psalm 34:8 *O taste and see that the LORD is good; blessed is the man that trusteth in him.*

When you taste God, you desire more of him, more of his word. Feed me Jesus, Feed me Jesus, desiring the sincere milk of the Word.

Leviticus 4:31 And he shall take away all the fat thereof, as the fat is taken away from off the sacrifice of peace offerings; an d the priest shall burn it upon the altar for a sweet smelling savour unto the LORD, and the priest shall make an atonement for him and it shall be forgiven him.

To touch the Lord is to draw nigh to him and he will draw nigh to you. Being in God's presence you can feel how much he loves and care for you.

SEEK THE KINGDOM

*S*eek *ye the kingdom of God and his Righteousness all other things shall be added unto you. Matthew 6:33*
　　Your timing is not God's timing. You must wait up him to act upon your life to give instruction to make things happen that will not fail. Ex 14:14

> **seek** (sēk) *v.* **sought** (sôt), **seek·ing, seeks.** *--tr.* **1.** To try to locate or discover; search for. **2.** To endeavor to obtain or reach. **3.** To go to or toward. **4.** To inquire for; request. **5.** To try; endeavor. **6.** *Obsolete.* To explore. *--intr.* To make a search or an investigation. (American Heritage Dictionary)

When you seek first, you are searching, going toward God, as God has already told us that if we draw nigh to him, he will draw nigh to us. So go after God and his righteousness, those things which is right and all the other things will be added. I'm reminded of a young lady whom God had given this scripture to and she had to go after God with all her heart, soul, mind and strength. Everything had to be laid down, even, how she thought. God had to take her mind and give her a mind of him. It was then no more I but Christ she stated. Everything she once knew, she knew no more, God had came in and gave her the mind of Christ. It took separating from people, places and things. Given up all for Christ, she was sincerely going after God, searching for the only one who could heal her from brokenness, deliver her from past mistakes and set her free, to be all she could be for her Saviour, Master, Redeemer and Maker. Her healing processed began with scriptures Psalm 19:12 Who can understand his errors? Cleanse thou me from my secret fault. As she was riding from shopping, God spoke to her and revealed all her errors and even those secret faults, things that had been hurting her for years from childhood, to adult, as a mother and Wife. God started working on her heart, so that he would have her undivided attention. As she confessed her hurt, disappointment, struggle, losses and all those secret things that had attached themselves to her, weighs begin to fall off her and she prayed, prayed and prayed. So whatever is broken in you seek God.

God wants you to give him a life, you must die in the Lord to receive eternal life from God. So, take on the spirit of God where he can use you. PRAISE GOD.

A CRUMB

Matthew 15:24:28 But he answered and said, I am not sent but unto the lost sheep of the house of Israel. Then came she and worshipped him, saying, Lord, help me. But he answered and said, It is not meet to take the children's bread, and to cast it to dogs. And she said, Truth, Lord: yet the dogs eat of the crumbs which fall from their master's table. Then Jesus answered and said unto her, O woman, great is thy faith: be it unto thee even as thou wilt. And her daughter was made whole from that very hour.

One crumb of God word is more than the whole loaf. You must eat of the crumb which fall from the table which is the word. Ask God to fill your cup and let it over flow with the blessings that he has in store for you. God's crumb is better than man's bread. *Matthew 5:6 Blessed are they which do hunger and thirst after righteousness, for they shall be filled.* You can receive if you have faith—know without faith it is impossible to please God. *Hebrew 11:6 But without faith it is impossible to please him: for he that cometh to God must believe that he is, and that he is a rewarder of them that diligently seek him.*

There are times in your life when you need God to do something extraordinary in your life or situation. You can worshipped God and get your answer, get your miracle but you have to persistent in your asking like the Syrophenician woman who asked Jesus to heal her daughter, she agreed with the Word, she trust the Word, she believe the Word and the Word(Jesus) move on her behalf.

CONQUERING THE MIND

oman 12:1-2 *I beseech you therefore brethren, by the mercies of God that ye present your bodies a living sacrifice, holy acceptable unto God which is your reasonable service. And be not conformed to this world, but be ye transformed by the renewing of your mind, that ye may prove what is that good, and acceptable, and perfect, will of God.*

There are some people who thinks about the plan God has for us and we will try to get in the plan- spiritual save, mind – saved. We have to be rebuilt to the things of God. " A Renewed Mind. It's your decision to become better, put yourself in position to receive, come out as a yield sign, deny(mortify the flesh) and follow him(Jesus). You got to get out of the way, you must be holy and that mean that which is holy, anything that is connected will destroy that which is unholy.

It's not in how you dress but you must put on the nature of God. When you get Jesus on the inside the outside will change, there will be a change.

How do you really come God? We say come just has you are. You can't with an attitude; you have to come before God and be ye transformed by the renewing of mind. A change has to come. You may even say, What do I change? What I wear, people that I associate. The mind must be renewed that you might prove what is really good and holy in the sight of the Lord Jesus Christ.

Until you get in the presence of God and empty out all the old things, repent and accept God into your life, you will not change. It takes God to change and to renew your mind. There is a process, so don't get discourage in the process, stay faithful and committed to what you want God to do in you, through you and around you. Read the word of God daily, speak the things of God and believe.

WAIT ON GOD

A Word from the Lord

In my Father house are many mansions: if it were not so, I would have told you. I go to prepare a place for you. John 14:2

You've been faithful over a few things but I said I will make you ruler over many. These are the words I heard God saying to me in the early morning hour. When you are going through and the enemy tries to weigh you down, Wait on God. God comfort my heart with what he have prepare for me heavenly and naturally. God said, my grace is sufficient for you, I shall give you peace in this life journey. These are the words that comforted me and gave me joy. I am not through blessings you says the Lord, I will give you victory in your going and coming, I shall give you long life and that I have now.

I had to believe what God was speaking to me, he covered every area of my life. You shall have what you desire, I'll do it for you said the Lord. His instruction to me was to stay prayerful, give me glory and no good thing shall I withhold from you. You shall stand in the presence of my people and they shall know that I'm you God who you trust. You are my servant, I shall use you to complete my work in time like these. I will manifest my vision to you to carry the mission that has been placed in your hands. **Wait on Me(God).** You shall bless your family and the children in need, they shall receive comfort in talking with you for my sake, you shall have power in your speech to reach the lost, they shall receive power to give me praise. I command you to stand boldly and don't be afraid of the power that I shall invest in you for my sake. I shall give you great power in you work for me in this life. PRAISE GOD.

You shall witness too many and they shall see the Christ in you. I'm not finish, I have much more for you to do in this world. PRAISE GOD

BEACH COMBER

*I*t's time to get naked before God, it's time to be real. We are people with different masks on in the Church.

Call Sin – Sin—get serious and repent
Naked -Not covered by clothing(*Webster's New Collegiate Dictionary*)
Attributes – Thought, motives

Why do it? The acts of the flesh, no control in self and not God, some have the I can't help it spirit.

We know the Eagle is real, don't be a chicken. We want to be an eagle, the eagle will mount up on wings and fly. He's flies as close to the sun, and we should get as close to God and soar high in him. *Isaiah 40:31 But they that wait upon the Lord shall renew their strength; they shall mount up with wings as eagles; they shall run, and not be weary; and they shall walk, and not faint.*

My mind pictures a man taking a stroll or a walk on the beach. We sometimes stroll or walk for many reason, such as health, to firm the body or even to seek a peace of mind. He will think about many things in life, circumstances and situations. The beach is a solemn place to bring all your thoughts to God, being real, taking off all things that's not of him, just get naked before him. You have no need to feel embarrassed or ashamed, it's just you and God.

He stated, he will never leave you or forsake you, he's there with you every step of the way. He's your help in the time of trouble. *Psalm 46:1 God is our refuge and strength, a very present help in trouble.*

Remember, you are not alone, if Jesus is your Savior, then he'll lead you into all truth. Now in your silent stroll on the beach, combing through all your life journeys that you have traveled, know that you have a savior that cares, a savior who loves you, he will fill all the gaps in your life. As you take this stroll of life which can be a tedious journey, make sure you have a clear view which leads to righteousness.

I took this stroll of life and he provided for me and my family. He cloth us, he put food on my table and provided shelter in the times of a storm. All you have to do is get naked, take off the mask –LET GO and LET GOD have his way in your life.

A little talk or walk with Jesus will make everything all right.

TAKING THE LIMIT OFF GOD

I was talking with Mother Lillie Riley and we realized that nothing has changed, we are just living in a different generation. Society has called this generation the X-generation, what a mistake, spoken over the lives of our younger generation. *Proverbs 18:21 Death and Life are in the power the tongue; an they that love it shall eat the fruit thereof.* Train up a child in the way he should go, for when he is older he will not depart from it. *Roman 8:1, Therefore, there is no condemnation to them which are in Christ Jesus who walk not after the flesh but the spirit. Also, Roman 8:28 For we know that all things work together for good to them that love God to them that are called according to his purpose.*

Although we go through trials and tribulation, we know God will rescue us and deliver us from all things. As God was speaking to me, I realized we as a people of the Lord, need to know that God is our TOTAL source. He's our ALL and ALL. *Psalm 34:19 Many are the afflictions of the righteous: but the Lord delivereth him out of them all.*

He will continue to deliver us, no matter what the problem is, he will deliver us. *Hebrew 4:15 says, For we have not an high priest which cannot be touched with feeling of our infirmities; but was in all points tempted like as we are, yet without sin.* If Jesus went through, so will we. Jesus lived here on this earth for 33 years, that was the generation that his father ordained for him to go through, all the suffering he experienced, he was found doing his father business.

He knew his assignment, he has the assurance of his father, no limit, he knew if he asked it, his father will do it.

This generation can live for God, but we must remained faithful to him and compel them, that the wages of sin is death but the gift of God is eternal life.

Roman 8: 6, 9 For to be carnally minded is death but to be spiritually minded is life and peace. But ye are not in the flesh, but in the spirit. If so be that the spirit of God dwell in you. Now if any man have not the Spirit of Christ, he is none of his.

Our young people today need to see us living the life that Jesus talked about and lived. We need to live the life before them. Jesus was faithful and committed to his Father and his assignment. No matter how Satan tried to attack him, he stood. Jesus said, I am the way, the truth and the life no man shall see the father unless he come through me. It's in Christ. Jesus spoke to the disciple with promise, if you have faith as small as a mustard seed, you can say to this mountain move from here to there and it will move.

Job 23:10 He knoweth the way that I may take; when he tried me I shall come forth as pure gold. 1ˢᵗ Samuel 12:23 I will teach you the good and rightway. Roman 8:29-31 For whom he did foreknow he also did predestinate to be conformed to the image of his Son, that he might be the firstborn among many brethren.

Moreover whom he did predestinate, them he also call: and whom he called, them he also justified: and whom he justified, them he also glorified. What shall we then say to these things? If God be for us, who can be against us.

SPIRITUAL WARFARE

*E*phesians 6:12 For we wrestle not against flesh and blood, but against principalities, against powers, against the ruler of darkness of this world, against spiritual wickedness in high places.

We sometimes struggle with the sin of omission and the sin commission, but we do not wrestle with flesh and blood. It's not the people that we fight against, instead it's the enemy who wants to keep us bound in every area of our lives.

Spiritual - that which originate from God or pertained to God's unique work in the universe and in the lives of the believers. (Nelson Bible Reference Companion)

Warfare – active military conflict.

As a believer in God's word, we are in an active conflict with the enemy, he's constantly trying to stop us from doing what God says to do. Take your stand with God. You must make a firm decision, no matter what the enemy will try to feed you. *1st Corinthians 15:58 Therefore, my beloved brethren, be ye stedfast, unmoveable, always abounding in the work of the Lord, forasmuch as ye know that your labor is not in vain.*

So fight the good fight of faith, lean and depend on God. No matter what may come your way, always know that the enemy is defeated. Be free today and let your testimony help others conquer the works and the tricks of the enemy.

Deliverance is a covenant between you and God. You must choose between God and Satan. Who are you going to believe? Deliverance is a life process. We are striving for perfection through Jesus Christ.

The Holy Spirit will not move unless you have faith. We measure sin but God don't. Once you confess you must depend on God for total deliverance. He that covereth his sin will not prosper. The Holy Spirit will show you what you need to see and you can get free. Ask God to anoint you with the spirit of Discernment to see the things you need to confess. Then cast out the demons and send them into dry places where he can't operate in your life.

I MADE IT OVER

I can truly say, I made it over, through it all God brought me through. Sunshine and rain, talk about but I made it. I am a Holy Woman and a Woman of Excellence. Phillippians 1: 10 That ye may approve things that are excellent; that ye may be sincere and without offence till the day of Christ. I had to hear the instruction from my father and attend to know understanding. He taught me also and said unto me let thine heart retain my words, keep my commandment and live. And I'm living this day in the fullness of Him. Prov 12:26 The righteous is more excellent than his neighbor but the way of the seduced them. We have to be careful in all our endeavors because you may never know who is watching you, therefore, we must be an example of Holy women because we are role models, a creation, molded into the image of God in how likeness.

I'm reminded of Anna, she became the first christian missionary Read Luke 2: 36-38. Her name mean Grace and Favor, she served God with fasting and Praying. Without a doubt Anna was one of God own elect, which she would cry day and night until he heard her. It was not in some nook of the temple she prayed or in a corner where female only supplicated God, she would join with others openly in the presence of the congregation and pour out her soul audibly in the temple. We the women of must stand tall and open our eyes, listen with our ears and be led by god and do what is pleasing in the sight of the Lord.

We must learn how to crucify the flesh in order to serve God, more acceptably where he can use us. There are many women in the Bible that were women of excellent and made it over with obeying God and pour out to him. Deborah stood out amongst the wisest of all in the old testament,

Dorcas a Philantropist, she thought up ways to help. She was known for here care of widow and clothing the poor. Give God the glory for all he has brought you through. Some might say you couldn't and some might say you shouldn't,

But I MADE IT, THANK GOD, I MADE IT THROUGH